STEAMPUNK ABC

A Collection of Contraptions and Curiosities

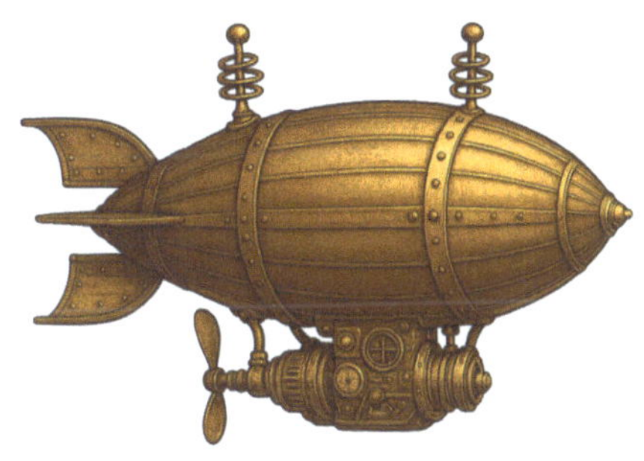

STEAMPUNK ABC

A Collection of Contraptions and Curiosities

Capt. James L. Paladin

Published by TGAF PRESS San Antonio, TX

ISBN: 979-8-9942922-0-4

Book Design by Capt. James L. Paladin

This book is dedicated to all the inquisitive children who dare to dream and create. Never give up.

A is for Airship

An amazing,
astounding,
astonishing
airship.

Abracadabra !

B is for Bicycle

A beautiful bright brass bicycle.
Bravo!

C is for Compass

Compass

A curiously cosmic copper compass. Cool!

D is for

Dragon

A dark,
dramatic,
dashing
dragon.
Danger!

E is for Engine

An enormous, enchanting, elegant engine. Encore!

F is for

Fan

A fancy,
fabulous,
futuristic
fan.
Fantastic!

G is for Goggles

A gift of gloriously geeky goggles. Golly!

H

is for
Helmet

A heavy,
hard-wired,
high-tech helmet.   Hooray!

I is for Iron

An imaginary but importantly impressive iron. Indeed!

J is for Jetpack

A jillion,
jeweled,
jet-powered
jetpacks.

Just joking!

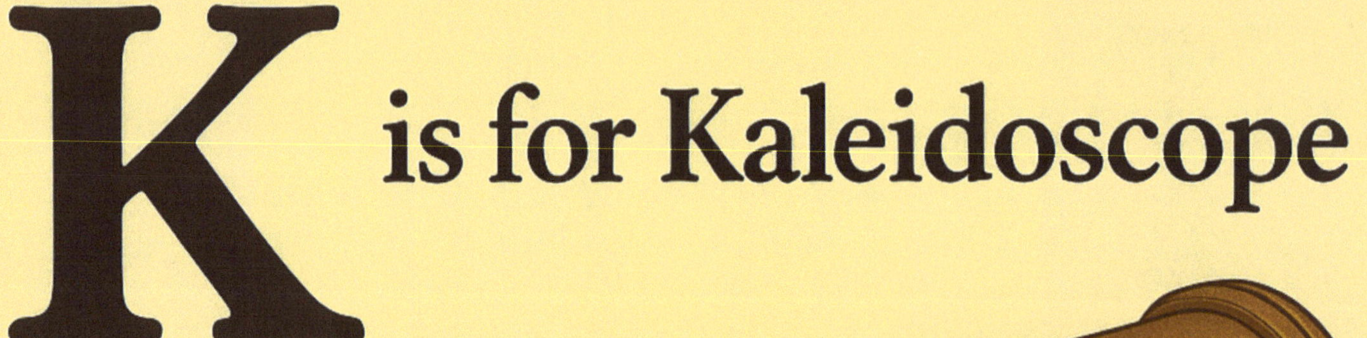

K is for Kaleidoscope

A kingly,
kinetic,
keepsake
kaleidoscope.

It's a keeper!

L is for Lamp

A large, luminous, lighted
lamp.
Lovely!

M
is for
Map

A mysterious,
mystifying,
metallic map.

Magical!

N is for Notebook

A nifty, novelty, noteworthy notebook. No snooping!

O

is for

Owl

An out-of-the-ordinary observant old owl.

Outstanding!

P is for Pickup truck

A powerful, picture-perfect
pickup truck.
Presto!

Q is for Queen Bee

A quick, quirky, quizzical queen bee.
Quite right!

R is for
Robot
A royal,
remarkably
retro robot.
Really!

S is for Snow Globe

A secret, spellbinding, sparkling snow globe.

Surprise!

T is for Telephone
A totally tricky tiptop
telephone. Terrific!

U

is for

Umbrella

An utterly unique
but useful Umbrella.

Unbelievable!

V is for Violin

A very valuable, varnished violin.
Voilá!

W is for Weather Balloon

A wayward, wandering, wind-blown weather balloon. Wild!

X is for X-Ray Fish

An XS, XL, or XXL
X-ray fish.
XOXOXO

Y is for Yo-yo

A yummy yellowish yo-yo just for you. Yahoo!

Z is for Zeppelin

A zippy, zigzagging,
zooming zeppelin.
Zounds!